i

saw

you

as

a

flower

ellen everett

i saw you as a flower

www.elleneverett.com

Cover design by Ellen Everett
Interior illustrations by Daria Maliarova and Martina Dobrev

ISBN: 978-0692097724

to those who have
loved me and believed in me
and to those
who have not

thank you

 there is a time for everything

pain.
tears.
losing.
missing.
aching.
emptiness.
loneliness.
abuse.
sadness.
heartbreak.

a time

to wither.

you held me so tight
that i left with your scent on my shirt
and that was the last thing
you ever gave me

i did not know
that simply
hearing someone
say your name
could make oceans
fill my tear ducts

you thought
i'd always be there

you thought
that once you had me
i was a permanent fixture—
a plant that did not need
watering or sunlight
to grow and thrive.

so you left me
in the darkness to wilt

and you ask where i went

i still remember
the last time
we made eye contact

my heart shudders
at the thought of it

the audacity
people have
to tell you
they love you

while knowing
it is only
their brain speaking
and not their heart

what do you do
when you both
love each other
but want different things

what do you do
when you both
crave light

but you want the sun
and he wants the moon

you have mastered
the art
of drowning people
without water

i want to believe
those three little words
but i cannot
because i feel alone
even when you are beside me

in every room
i look for you
even though
we may be
on opposite universes

i'm somewhere between
not knowing where you are
and *wanting to be there*

i would much rather
my limbs hurt
than my heart

why did you let me think i know you,
when i know you not?

the only person that i know
is the person that i thought
was telling the truth.

there's a shallowness inside your eyes
each time you look at me;

i used to be your ocean once,
but now i'm your dead sea.

i told you
that you were my sunlight
and ever since
i've been walking in
darkness

you must have wanted
someone else
to shine for

i like crooked noses
and crooked smiles

but not crooked hearts

are you okay
they ask

i respond
as quickly
as i can
so they will not
notice the earthquakes
in my voice
or the tsunamis
in my eyes
or the drought
in my heart

i'm a heartbreaker

i've broken my own heart
many times
because i'd rather be alone
than hold the hand of someone
who makes me forget
who i am
and that i even had a heart
to begin with

without you
i confuse the daytime
with night

it's always dark here

you love me in waves

he would give me the ocean

my heart is
either waning or waxing
and i am tired
of waiting
for it to be full

how do you go
from talking to me
every day
to
pretending
i was never there

*i had not prepared
to be invisible*

you open the door for me
only when they are watching
to tell them
that you put me first

but they do not see
my body shrivel
and my hands tremble
like an earthquake

they do not hear
the sound of my heart breaking
when you yell at me
and remind me
repeatedly
that i am not

you told me so many lies
that slowly
you began to forget the truth

i began to forget too

                    -manipulation

my head tells me
that we are okay—
this house
we built on the sand
will resist
the arms of the ocean

but the sands are
being loosened beneath us
by the waves
and my heart tells me
to run to the rocks
where i can build
something that will last

he told you he would
lay on the porch with you
and watch the fireflies dance

but instead
he met her on her porch steps
and with her, he danced

you saw them
and the fireflies lost their glow

-so did you

everything happens
for a reason
but i can't help myself
from wishing
that you were born
to love me

and like a funnel, you sifted
the finest pieces of my heart
until it was left paralyzed
and i wonder when
i will feel it
beat again

-numb

he loves me
he loves me not

he wants me
he wants me not

he sees me
he sees me not

he knows me
he knows me not

-falling out of love

how painful it is
for my brain to forget
what my heart longs to remember
and remember
what my heart longs to forget

i'm adrift.
you were my compass for direction,
but you had broken hands—
ones that wouldn't hold mine.

but they weren't afraid
to make bruises,
and that's not how hands
should be used and,
i didn't think you would do it.

you picked me from the earth
to be yours
and let me wilt

at the same time,
you left her in the garden
but nurtured her
with your love
and affection
that i needed

i withered
wishing
i was her

you told me
to let down my hair
but you cringed
as you felt it
between your fingertips

you told me to love myself
but then showed me
why i shouldn't

do you love me
he asked

i told him no
while thinking
i always will

-saying goodbye to a best friend

the earth was too warm
for the snowflakes—
i watched them kiss its surface
and disappear

i couldn't help but wonder
if i was too warm for you

you touched me
and i haven't seen you since

i filled my room
with dreamcatchers
to keep
the bad dreams away

and yet
you are always
waiting for me
in my sleep
determined to haunt me

you drink nectar
with the hummingbirds
but prey with the vultures
and you wonder why
you cannot be trusted

-you are who you are with

you screamed at me
for hours
and somehow
i am the one
apologizing

i'm just trying to
silence the noise

when you said goodbye
my heart left with you

and it is so hard
to live
with only a brain

i loved you
because you awoke
a wildfire in me
that flickered behind my retinas
and made my eyes see
the world
with a little more light

how could you
light a fire in me
and extinguish it
without warning

you showed me
a kindness
that i had never
been shown before

how both blessed
and cursed i am
to have received it
and had it taken away

your words are piercing me like needles
that are breaking through my skin.
from the outside i seem numb,
but i'm stinging from within.

i tell myself that words can't cut me,
but yours are like a group of knives—
and they're whittling at my heartstrings,
shaving what i thought was mine.

sometimes they cut so deeply,
my heartstrings are holding by a thread.
but your words can only carve so deep—
they'll never leave me dead.

here comes
the dull ache
my heart
is so
familiar with

you held me,
and i was afraid.
no one had ever wanted to hold me before

you tucked my hair behind my ears,
and i was afraid.
no one had ever looked at me like that before

you held my chin,
and i was afraid.
no one had ever gotten that close to me before

and i should have known
that you weren't afraid to leave.
no one had ever stayed before

what hurts the most
is seeing the girls
you choose after me
beside you
for other reasons
than loving your heart

and again
i go to bed early
because it hurts too much
to stay awake
and think about
how you aren't here

the only place
i can be with you
is in my dreams

oh how difficult
it is
to balance

celebrating
and mourning
the time you had with someone

i didn't know words
could be so confusing
and make me feel like
i'm always losing—
i'm under the impression
that you were just using them
to make me think
you were something
you knew you weren't

i wish that i could
exfoliate you
from my heart
like you
did with me

but you are rooted much deeper
than its surface
and by the time i could shed
enough layers
to rid myself of you
there would be
only a little
of my heart left

and i'm not sure
if hearts can grow back

why do i
love so strongly
but break
like porcelain

i hang my head
and let my hair and tears
fall
towards
the
ground

i am a weeping willow

the days before
my heart
was held in
careless hands
i used to
look forward
to my future

now i am
suffocated by the fear
that no one
could ever love me

you think you have a way with words,
but, my dear, your silver tongue

is what drove a wedge between
who we were hoping to become.

sometimes
i am
not the princess—
i am the dragon

and every now and then
i burn myself
with my own fire

you had a sweetness
that was artificial

but how could
i have known
when
your words
tasted like sugar

the sad thing is,

i forgot my real name
amongst
the mountain of names
you called me

i saw you as a flower;
your petals had a certain glow.
within a patch of dandelions,
i saw you as a rose.

but when i plucked you from the earth, my dear,
i watched your colors fade.
your ruby petals that once showed me love
became a shade of jade.

you spoke to me with bitter words,
and i saw you wilt before my eyes.
so when you shed your petals,
it was much less a surprise.

i saw you as a flower,
but now my eyes can see;
you're nothing but a thorn—
as for the flower, it was me.

it would
be easier
if i could just
unlove you

the difference between
you and i is,

you wanted
to be intimate with
a body
and i wanted
to be intimate with
a heart

when the sun
goes down,
it has to know
the moon
will renew its light.

if i'm the sun,
i need to know,
where is my moon at night?

there were no sadder eyes
than the ones
of the girl
who let a boy
convince her
that she was not beautiful

he leaves bruises
on your skin
and you still
believe that
he loves you

*he has left bruises
on your mind too*

you picked me up
like a dandelion
and ripped off
my wishes

each night
when i fall asleep
      it is images of you
      thoughts of you
      moments of you
that flood my mind

and i cannot decide
whether to call them
dreams
or
nightmares

i know
it is not me
that you miss

just a hand
to hold.
an ear
to listen.
a good morning
and goodnight.

a flower
to kill.

i have loved
and i have loved
until i cannot
love anymore
and somehow
i still find
more love in me
to love with

how am i
supposed to forget you
when it is
your flowers
that are blooming
from my organs

healing.
rising.
self-worth.
overcoming.
learning.
striving.
self-betterment.
happiness.
believing.
thriving.

a time

to grow.

we may have dark nights

but the sun will rise to remind us
that *so will we*

in a blue vase
on my dresser
the flowers you gave me
hang their heads

you are gone
but these wilted flowers
have kept you with me

today i threw them out
and i found myself
letting you go

-acceptance

you are
the best flower
i know

-my nana's words
as she handed me a bouquet

i love
the sun too much
to give it up
for someone
who is nocturnal

i was wrong to mistake you for oxygen—
to think that i needed you to live.

because you were actually
the
       very
            element
                  that
                        suffocated
                                me.

-you're gone and i can breathe again

81

writing is about
shedding your shield
and allowing yourself
to be vulnerable

it is about forcing yourself
to confront your demons
and to let yourself feel

-this is also what healing is about

you were alive
before
you met him

you are still alive
now that
you are strangers again

i hope that you never
tell yourself
that you must slip off your dress
to feel loved
or to be beautiful
or to have worth
because your beauty is not skin-deep—
it is much more than that

and one day
someone will fall in love
with your laughter
and with the way
their universe stands still
when you breathe

i refuse to look behind me
at the ones who chose
to take my heart
and throw it
into the flames

i will not be your pillar of salt

i let the sun
give me freckles
so i could share
a piece of sunshine
with someone
in the dark

remember that
just because
the girl beside you
is beautiful

does not mean
that you are
not

when i am broken-hearted
i think about my Jesus—

a crown of thorns.
His back torn.
nails piercing His hands and feet.
Him watching as His loved ones weep.
His blood trickling.
His breath faltering.
a cross standing.
a body hanging.
a man dying.
a God saving.

when i am broken-hearted
i think about my Jesus—

and i remember
that my Jesus was thinking about me

-and He still is

you have
the whole world
there for you

waiting to be seen

i believe in miracles,
and i hope that you do too.

because if you don't believe that they exist,
then you don't believe in *you.*

you scorch the sun
with your ultraviolent eyes
and you bend the earth
with your footsteps

stars fall from the sky
at the sight of your smile
and the moon itself
gleams from the light
that you radiate

you generate ocean waves
with your heartbeat
and the mountains quiver
at the sound of your voice

you breathe
and the wind marvels
at how powerful you are

i cannot make
everybody happy

i am only a person

-and that is okay

ellen everett

there is no shame in emotion

even the earth cries
so its flowers can grow

be a light
that doesn't cast shadows
on anyone

have a smile
that shines
for everyone

and create a happiness
that can be taken by
no one

poetry is the music
for those
who cannot sing

years ago
i remember praying
for you to change

today
i thank God
for saying no

and for deciding to
change me instead

laughter is the music
in a world
full of too much silence

and the silence
in a world
full of too much noise

we are all flowers
underneath the same sun

we bloom
in an array of
colors.
shapes.
sizes.

-this is what makes the garden so beautiful

thank you
for teaching me
to love myself

i had to
when i realized
that you didn't

time doesn't wait on us;
it doesn't pause for us to play.
it doesn't stop for us to complete our dreams;
it moves forward either way.

it doesn't press rewind;
a moment passed is a moment lost.
if you didn't speak your heart,
then regret will be the cost.

time goes on forever,
but our time will surely end.
if you don't make the most of the time you have,
then time is not your friend.

do not open your heart
to negativity

do not let thorns
take up space
where your flowers could grow

think what you wish
to think about me

but the birds still sing
to me each morning
and the sun awakens
to kiss my skin
and the earth spins
just to see where my feet
will choose to wander

and i am loved

she became so free
the birds themselves
envied her wings

i hope that you never know
what it feels like
to brush your teeth
with the bathroom lights off
because the
reflection in the mirror
deems itself
unworthy to be seen

turn the lights on

you are a lighthouse.
you are meant to
pierce through the darkness.

you do not shine so bright
not to be seen

you have been taught
to reach for the stars
but i hope you learn
to chase the moon instead

it shines brighter

we will all meet sadness
and look it in the eyes

but it is up to us
to put one foot
ahead of the other
and continue walking
until we meet happiness

-and there we will choose to stay

make it your goal
this year
to walk into every room
with a smile on your face
and watch how much
your life will change

-for the better

let us live like flowers

wild and beautiful
and drenched in sun

do not let your infatuation
blind you
from seeing
flaws in someone

you always choose
to see good in people—
even the ones
who are not good

pretty flaws
can still be fatal.
not everyone's sky
is as blue as yours

i am clothed in sun
and cannot welcome
someone who is
afraid of light

-self-worth

i am leaving my mistakes
behind me
as shadows of who i was
but not of who i will become

that is the beautiful thing
about shadows
they will always fall behind you
when you face the sun

and to the sun
i am running

being brave
does not mean
that you live unafraid

but rather
that you continue to speak
even when
your voice is shaking

dear you,

you fixate on
your face and body
because you want people
to fall in love
with your beauty

and you do not understand
why people use you
as a house
instead of home

signed,
your heart

it is okay
to not have
the same talents
as someone else

*it takes both
raindrops and sunbeams
for flowers to grow*

there is
a songbird inside of you
flapping its wings
against its cage

but i cannot
set it free for you
and maybe you would
if you saw
what i see in you

point your telescopes
to the universe,
and admire how it never ends.

then remember this universe around you,
is nothing compared to
your universe *within.*

we dream of being
loved like gold
but we settle
for someone who
loves us like silver
and we wonder
why we tarnish

   -*victimizing ourselves*

do not let the world
steal your joy

it is good at that
*but you are better
than to let it*

my dreams are
bigger than the galaxies
and i will achieve them
one star at a time
until the universe
isn't big enough
for all that i will do

do not let
a hundred gray skies
erase your memory
of the blue ones

they will come

why do
you cringe
when you look
at yourself
in the mirror

don't you see
the stardust
in your eyes

the beautiful thing about humans
is that we are
living and dying
simultaneously

but i choose to focus
only on the living

our
hearts
will
burn
down
like
forests

but come back
like the garden of eden

we can
move mountains
with our words
so here i am
speaking

and i cannot wait
to watch the mountains
jump with excitement

you are
who your friends are
so i surrounded myself
with wildflowers

speak only words
as sweet
as the honeysuckles
and you will always
be surrounded
by pleasant company

holding on
to the hope
that he will come back
is preventing you
from letting go
and moving on
to someone better

*you cannot hold on
and let go at the same time*

like a roll of film,
it is in darkness
that you develop
your colors

why do we
feel weak
when we see
how strong
others are

radiate so much positivity
that the sun
rises each morning
to compete
with your light

even if i am
stripped
of everything
i will not
be nothing

i will always be
something

you dropped my heart
in quicksand
assuming it would sink

you underestimate
the power
my heart has
to withstand adversity

i have always hated this ribcage
for protruding
from my skin
but maybe it is
just pleading to be recognized
and commended
for all the times
it has protected my heart
and kept it in place
when it was weary

i am sorry for hating you
when you have done nothing
but love me

i have lost myself
many times

and
that
is
how
i
found
me

someone who
makes you feel
like a no one
is not
a someone
at all

we are afraid
to wander
outside of
our comfort zones

but if
we do not
open our shells
how are we
supposed to
find our pearls

speak to me
in lilacs and lace
for that is
the language
i know best

dear heart,

out of all
the time i spent
not loving myself
you did not
forsake me,
you did not
cease from beating

*thank you for not giving up
when i did*

today
is a beautiful day
to wake up
and love yourself

sometimes
the wrong person
may wear a halo
but darling,
you will know
an angel
when you meet one

chapters of your life
will end
but you have
multitudes of pages
left in your book

and so many books after that

darling
your petals
are too lovely
to be in the shade
where he keeps you

if i become
anything in my lifetime
let it be the wind

what a wondrous thing
to be felt
without being seen

i saw you as a flower

your sad tears
will become
happy tears

and the sad ones
will all make sense

144

in fourth grade
a girl
gave me fifty cents
and said

i plant some seeds
and watch them grow

if she only knew
it wasn't just fifty cents
she gave me that day,
but also
an outlook on life
that has
grown me gardens

loving.
affection.
feelings.
passion.
caring.
loyalty.
infatuation.
commitment.
giving.
uniting.

a time

to blossom.

i heard that you like working puzzles,
so here's this jigsaw i call my heart.
it comes in a million broken pieces,
so i hope that you are smart.

but when you put the final piece in place,
i hope you put me on the wall as art.
because i don't want for you to build me up,
just to take me back apart.

to my gardener:

before i met you
i loved flowers

and now
you plant kisses on my forehead
and roses bloom in my soul

i'm so lucky to be your garden

he handed her fake flowers
and said

i'll love you till the last flower dies

-eternity

hold my hand
for the spaces between
my fingers
long to be filled

hold my body
for these fragile bones
long to feel protected

hold my heart
for its tattered hull
longs to collapse
into your clean soul

when it comes to you
i am adrift

floating in circles
without a compass

no matter where
my feet go
my heart
will always
stay with you

oh
the love
i would give you
if you
would let me

i hope that you like winter,
because frost is blanketing my heart.

and i hope that i like spring,
because i'm melting in your arms.

when the day comes
that we meet,
know that i
have prayed every night
to find you

-to my soulmate

to describe you
is like trying to
imagine a new color
and i realize

some things are
too beautiful
to make sense of

you have taught
my clumsy heart
how to dance

if you're looking for forever,
i'll take the batteries out of my clocks.
so that we'll be stuck inside this moment,
as if time had really stopped.

i would tell you i love you every second,
except here, seconds do not exist.
so i'll say i love you with each breath,
with each smile, with each kiss.

and when i die, you can crank your watch,
restart your clocks, begin the time.
and know that we were infinite
in the moment that you were mine.

with one look
we knew
love had found us

*the earth saw it,
and trembled*

you cannot tell me
that you can only love someone
after a certain amount of time has passed

love has no time limits
or time frames

-*God loved me before i even existed*

how easy it is for me
to find myself lost in your eyes
for they are the color
of the oceans

like a sea of waves
my stomach tosses and turns
when i look into them

and somehow i fear
the calm that will come
when i look away

the sky is my favorite when
her horizon blushes and
her cheeks are flushed
with orchid and lavender

i wonder if the sky smiles too
and gazes in awe and admiration
when she sees
my cheeks are flushed
with orchid and lavender

she has to know
i think to myself

that my eyes have seen him—
the one who makes
my heart flutter
and my skin burst with color

i can't wear my heart
on my sleeve
because my heart
is in your hands

the world is cold
and frigid are its people

but in you i find warmth—
a safe haven,
a place of comfort,
the center of my happiness

dearest,
you are my equator

my love for you is

boundless.
ceaseless.
constant.
deathless.
enduring.
eternal.
everlasting.
infinite.
limitless.
measureless.
unbroken.
undivided.
undying.
unfathomable.
unsurpassable.

and *without end*

you are the completion to me
and i did not know
that i was unfinished

                -*whole*

he doesn't notice
that even the stars
fall from the sky
to get a better view
of his light

there are stories in your eyes
and a purpose in your step

and i would love to be your adventure

like the earth
i am in orbit

and darling,
you are the sun

he is the night sky
and i hope
that in me
he sees constellations

i would gladly light up his universe

my heartstrings are like a harp,
and you pluck them one by one.
but when i look into your eyes,
my heart beats like a drum.

i am made up of piano keys,
and you play melodies on my skin.
but when you hug me, you hold me gently—
like i'm a violin.

my hands are like a tambourine,
and you hold them in your grasp.
you squeeze my fingers all too tightly,
just to hear me laugh.

i am like a wind chime,
and you are like the wind.
when we are both together,
music whistles from within.

my love is like a metronome—
always constant, always true.
but i didn't know what love was,
until the day that i met you.

isn't it beautiful
how the trees breathe
so we can exist

and we exist
so they can breathe

we give each other life

-it is the same with you and me

the moon
covered the sun
and the sky
turned black

i saw it with
my own eyes
but i am still convinced that
you are my eclipse

-my once in a lifetime

you are lightning.
i am thunder.

and i did not know
a storm
could be
so beautiful

you are the sweetness
in a bitter world
full of bitter-sweets

i drowned inside
your lapis eyes
your emerald laugh
and your ruby soul

and i want nothing more
than to be your diamond

when i am with you
my butterflies might not always
spread their wings and
fly around inside my stomach

but i still know
that they
are there

and that is what it means
to love someone

one day i will say
everything
i want to say
to you

      -timing

find someone
who doesn't just
give you flowers

the right person
will cause gardens
to bloom
from your soul

i am not electric
yet you light me up
with just
one touch

you fumble
with your words
and trip
over your ungraceful sentences

you don't always
know what to say
or how to say it

how nice it is
to know someone
who doesn't pretend
to know
all the answers

she calls me
her miracle
but it was her body
not mine
that was ripped apart
so i could live

-a mother's love

you didn't
love her today
because you thought
i can love her tomorrow

now tomorrow is here
and you miss her
because she found someone
who loves her regardless
of what day it is

185

my tone-deaf heart
sings symphonies
for you

you knew
my heart was stone
but you planted seeds
between the cracks

and when the spring came,
sprouting up
were flowers
in colors
the rainbow
had never seen before

your energy
is enough
to light up
every city

-infectious

love is not extinct
or endangered
and like spring
it will come to us
and bring us warmth
even after
the coldest winters

how is it that
even your rainstorms
look like
sunshine

ellen everett

i was created
to breathe

yet you insist upon
taking
my breath away

over and over again

all it took
was one glimpse
into your world

for mine
to become
a revolving door of

you

you

you

you

you

his eyes
are mirrors
that reflect
the sunbeams
in his heart

are   the
          . .   . .
you   rainbow
. . .   .
. . .   .
. . .   .
. . .   .
                          . . . .
after   . . . .
all
                          this
                          rain

me
noticing
you
noticing
me
noticing
you

we are trapped
in an infinite circle
of wanting each other

loving you
is like being swept
into a black hole
and it is impossible
to escape
your gravity

let me tiptoe
down
the hallways
of your mind

you sing
love songs to me
with your eyes

until the oceans dry up,
and the evergreens lose their color

until the sun forgets to shine,
and the birds can't remember how to sing

until the world isn't round,
and all of the stars fall out of the sky

i will love you

if you cannot tell already, i love flowers. for me, they have always been a message of positivity. what appears to be such a fragile little thing has the strength to withstand so much. through wind, rain, and storms, they are still able to grow and thrive as something beautiful. and so can we, even when the odds are against us. remember this as you go through your days.

much love,
ellen